Filthy Loot would like to thank Joe Koch, Kyle Winkler, Charlene Elslby, O F Cieri, and all the people responsabile (and who attended) the 2023 VoidCon in Huntington, WV for inspiring this collection of essays.

LIKE YOU NEVER HAD WINGS
Copyright © 2024 by their individual authors
Book & cover design by Ira Rat

This is a work of fiction. Names, characters, businesses, places, events, locales, and incidents are either the products of the author's imagination or used in a fictitious manner. Any resemblance to actual persons, living or dead, or actual events is purely coincidental.

This book may not be reproduced in whole or in part, except for the inclusion of brief quotations in a review, without permission in writing from the author or publisher. No part of this publication may be reproduced, stored in or introduced into retrieval system, or transmitted, in any form, or by any means (electronic, mechanical, photocopying, recording, or otherwise), without prior permission of the publisher.

Requests for permission should be directed to
eyerarat@gmail.com

FIRST EDITION

CONTROL

LIKE YOU NEVER HAD WINGS

JOE KOCH - 05

KYLE WINKLER - 33

CHARLENE ELSBY - 63

filthyloot.com

GOD, I FEEL MURDER TONIGHT: TRAUMA, TRANSFORMATION, AND BEYOND THE NORMAL IN HORROR

JOE KOCH

Let's begin with fairy tales, those oral precursors of our modern written horror stories originating more or less around the eighteenth century. Fairy tales are older than horror, as old as language and myth, so let's start with "The Frog Prince," a tale so ubiquitous it's entered the mental canon of people who've never even read it.

"You have to kiss a lot of frogs" we say to reassure the lonely that failure in the wilds of dating and romance is normal, or to give ourselves a boost when frustrated or unsatisfied by love. The cliché is usefully dismissive. We don't have to directly engage with grief or answer anyone's insistent, monotonous pleas as to why they never succeed. Good for us! We're not concerned with the abandoned heart's pathetic yearnings. We're here to talk about transformation in horror.

The saying represents a transformation of the fairy tale itself. Like playing a child's game of telephone, the message repeated in whispers, misheard and misremembered multiple times from person to person, the truism "You've got to kiss a lot of frogs" has lost the original plot. Most people incorrectly recall that the prince is cured of his amphibious enchantment by the princess bestowing a kiss. But go back to the original transcription of the oral tale, and you'll find the princess spoiled rotten and pushed past the brink of rage when the slimy frog cuddles up next to her in bed. She flies into a murderous tantrum, grabbing the small, soft-bodied creature and hurling it into the wall. It splatters like roadkill on impact, crushed to death.

In the very next moment, as the dead frog falls, a charming golden-haired prince lands on her bed. Happy ever after time ensues, at least for that first night, with its surprise bridegroom and suggestively stained sheets. Fairy tales tend to gloss over the more complicated drudgeries of romance beyond the first kiss, or in this case, beyond the first kill.

Many other folktales, mythical legends, and fairy tales involve enchantments that will only be cured by murder or dismemberment of an animal. While the frog prince chooses suicide by princess, other tales often lack comic overtones and slapstick violence. Typically, a young adventurer is tasked with killing a beloved magical creature that's rescued them, served them faithfully, or endured great hardship in their stead. Ignorance of the true purpose of this compulsory assault is essential for the spell to be broken. The future murderer swears under duress to behead or burn or scatter the parts of their faithful companion when the animal (who can, of course, talk) names this task as the only act of gratitude they will accept.

If such-and-such happens, do this. The precipitating event is so unlikely, or so distant from the would-be murderer's limited life experience, that it seems absurd or impossible, and they agree jovially, humoring the strange helper. They're too naïve to think they'll ever have to keep up their end of the bargain, too innocent to believe that the worst case scenario could come to pass. Inevitably, it does.

The world we live in would be a much more blood-stained place if our frustrated singles approached the dating scene with folkloric accuracy. Adopting the motto "You have to kill a lot of frogs" to improve the playing field might clear it of extraneous gold-diggers and disingenuous lotharios, but acting out the primal urges behind fairy tale and myth risks dire peril. Our naïve would-be murderer fears prosecution, perhaps unaware of the more monstrous effects of their quest: the fact of pain forever carried by survivors, the irreversible ruination of health and relationships, and the trauma radiating throughout their entire community for years after the event. Furthermore, our potential lover/killer must consider the murderer's own burden of knowledge, and the potential development of guilt, self-loathing, and loss of affect. An act of killing self-eviscerates, clearing a blank space inside like a blasted field where no emotions can grow. This, perhaps, is why our preferred slasher villain/hero of modern horror films is a faceless cipher who wears a mask.

Shapeshifting from archaic fairy tale to woeful lover to incomprehensible executioner hinges here upon playing irresponsible games with desire in order to embrace the atrocity at its core. We're all just so much temporarily animated dead meat, aren't we? And what greater trauma exists than death?

Many do, and in an unfortunately stunning and shocking array. Death in horror, however, means something other than the end.

Allegorically, the character of Death (in magical systems, alchemy, legends, tarot, and so on) symbolizes transformation. This points toward the idea that trauma is an essential component of shapeshifting and apotheosis. While death may be welcomed or peaceful rather than violent and loathed, death is nevertheless always a complete and final loss of physical autonomy and an entire erasure of individual psychological stability. Death's transformation will always remain unknowable. While we can only dance fitfully around its implications like cheerful hooded skeletons in a medieval woodcut, we might as well decide not to mope and follow in the footsteps of our skinless friends from the Dark Ages. Let's have a little fun circling this vast chasm of the unknown before we fall in forever and vanish.

We can have a little death, as a treat, to use a popular meme format. Of course the *little death*, translated from the French phrase *la petite mort*, became a euphemism for orgasm around the same time psychoanalysis emerged in Europe during the late nineteenth century. Notorious for mixing up sex and death, psychoanalysis changed the history of human thought by positing the existence of the subconscious, that murky place within us full of complicated, unknowable needs, ideas, and motivations that we can only pretend to comprehend. It's almost like a hidden chunk of death we all carry within us, a chip off the old void commandeering our dreams, rages, and most passionate desires.

Before we delve too deep into Freudian technicalities, it's worth noting that Freud's faulty patriarchal assumptions about gender and parent-child dynamics have been critiqued and largely discredited by modern practitioners. His seduction theory blamed victims of childhood trauma for the abuse they endured, encouraged false memories in others, pathologizing the survival response and re-traumatizing patients during treatment. Contemporary trauma-informed therapies focus on validating the health and sanity of early protective reactions essential to surviving immediate danger, and then work to place them where they belong in a person's history, discontinuing (through awareness, embodiment, and practice) these automatic emotional habits that are compulsively reenacted in the present.

Modern therapies arise from a model of health rather than illness, but old-school psychoanalysis with its dreams and forbidden desires and heady symbolism certainly has a delicious drama to it. Incest and patricide, oh my; and isn't drama exactly what we need for a good horror tale? Freud borrowed heavily from myth, legend, and poetry in his attempts to map the workings of the unconscious. We're following suit as we talk about horror, trauma, and transformation from princes to frogs, reversing enchantments, and achieving a changed form through violence. Unlike Freud, however, we're not keeping our sex and death separate.

Any horror fan intuitively understands the emotional resonance and interrelationship between Eros and Thanatos, the seemingly opposite instincts of libido and death drive. Loss of self is a key connector, but that doesn't fully explain the heightened effect of titillation (or scandalized offense) readers experience when we bounce sex and death off of one another in a text. There's only so much self a person can lose, after all. The possibility of transformation, of a sudden, involuntary, and unchangeable change is the real thrill—or threat—at work when we rub death and sex together hard enough to make The Juice.

The Juice happens in those moments of writerly epiphany, often accompanied by inappropriate cackling, when you know you've really gone too far. You realize you must be one sick fuck, and it fills you with perverse delight. Part of you knows you should stop. Your teacher or spouse or grandma wouldn't approve. But if you're any good at your job, you'll keep going, because your task is to show your reader the unthinkable. Or, better yet, to lead them closer and closer to the unthinkable until you can drop them in the muck and make them think it.

It may sound cruel, but I promise they'll love you for it.

The desire to know the unknowable is foundational to horror as a genre and endemic in the will to transformation. It acknowledges boundaries without accepting them. The reader who comes to horror does not want to leave unchanged. We owe them enough brutalization, torment, and disturbing ambiguity to ruin their day.

For instance, if I were asked to expound on transformation as a technical aspect of my writing, I might cite word choices made for their unsettling placement, juxtaposition, and sound as much as slippery plot arcs and shifting points of view that defy nonchalant reading. You need to pay attention.

Not only will I position words, ideas, and images in combinations intended to make a reader uncertain and uncomfortable, I will treat the reader as complicit in the violent disturbance, holding them "hostage" (to quote one critic) while refusing to explain precisely where they are and exactly what has gone wrong.

At its very best, the horror is revealed in a sense of knowing that clicks in the reader's mind, even if the pieces of the story do not make logical sense. Something changes in them as they realize the horror is already happening. By the time they see it, it is too late to refuse the terrible and unwanted knowledge. Like the silent death of a cell, horror has been quietly at work, infecting them all along. Like life.

Life is, after all, utterly immersed in death. Transformation is such an integral part of our daily burden of drudgeries that we hardly notice it. If we did, we might go a little mad with the constant affront to our identity and existence. Every breath is another moment passing away, one more tiny increment bringing us closer to our personal expiration date. All these thoughts we're batting about for shits and giggles will soon short out and simply vanish. The brain is part of the body and our bodies have one job: to kill us.

This trauma is happening right now. You are trapped inside a body, and bodies are genetically programmed to die, to rot. Parts of them fall out or flake away, trimmed, filed, and scrubbed off as we expire and mutate a little bit more each day. We regrow our cells slower and slower as we age. The integrity of our chromosomes breaks down. The very waste from our living bodies would suffocate us were it not for the robust action of colonies of microorganisms that feast on us. We would drown in our own garbage and feces were it not for insects carrying our copious biohazards away. Physical life is an interlocking process of continuous transformations.

To suggest transformation is possible confirms our impermanence. Horror simply amplifies the creeping truth. This is why the slasher genre fails to horrify. Our faceless hero-villain who looms up from the shadows will take you out in one swift chop, stab, or garroting.

The imaginative diversity and speed of the murders punctuates a necessarily mundane narrative with a slapstick effect, hardly encouraging the viewer or victim to ruminate on death and decay. Even for our final girl or boy who possesses knowledge of the killer, all action takes place during the hunt, and ends with escape, or the death of the murderer. Don't worry, though; he'll be back. They always come back, to the delight of fans who want thrills in denial of the true horror that has been quietly at work in our cells as we rotted for two hours while watching the film.

The real horror starts after the fake death and structural formula has played out. The final boy or girl (slashers seem too rudimentary to cope with transgender, nonbinary, genderless, or genderfluid characters unless, of course, they're demonized as the psychotic assassin) must now live with the slaughter they have witnessed and evaded. Furthermore, they must do so in the absence of the friends, family, and lovers whose mangled corpses litter the campground or neighborhood which was once a comforting, familiar, reliable place.

The killer is gone, but the world is a mess. When the slasher ends, transformation begins. As we move beyond the slasher, we experience real horror, an irreversible transformation of self that lingers like a haunting.

If we've been paying close attention, this change is nothing new. The world we inhabit was always in ruins. Horror simply gives us a fictionalized space where we can take off our blinders for a moment and experience the constant flux of existence as it really is, rotting, changing, gasping for breath, and collapsing into entropy as the planets work their way toward a future collision that will burn down the heavens and take our silly planet and our futile lives with it.

But what of our lone cipher, our masked nobody tasked with unsettling the illusions of certainty about ourselves and our world that we cling to in order to glibly function in everyday life? Allegorically, he is the unknowable face of death, isn't he? Yet within the confines of his genre, his actions are exceptionally knowable and predictable, unlike death. And here we could end our conversation about transformation in horror, on this didactic—and therefore reassuring—conundrum, except for the fact that allegories and symbols don't really exist. Murderers, however, are all too real.

Like the final boy or girl, we not only know this, but we also bear our particular curse as horror fans to want to know more.

Some people can't resist peeling back the mask, can they?

In case you don't like what you see, here's fair warning to end this awkward and disorganized attempt at an essay right now, and enjoy your semiotic or ideological or hermeneutical or whatever-you-want-to-call-it final rest in the sweet arms of conceptual death.

It was all a story, a movie, a bad dream. Who wants a fiction writer to propose facts, anyway? A horror writer, no less; the most heinous of liars! When you've lived as long as I have and experienced the way facts change across decades when viewed through different scientific, academic, and societal lenses, you come to realize objectivity is yet another illusion. Every fact is based on perception, and perceptions accrue from evidence collected through bodily senses and organized in the tender organ we call the brain. Our thoughts and consciousness are made of chemicals and electrical impulses tied to this impermanent and mutable thing we call the body.

You remember the body, don't you? It's the thing that wants to kill us.

I'm not sure how far you're willing to go with your transformation, what degree of extremity you'll accept. However, transformations in horror aren't typically contingent upon acceptance, are they? The slasher chops, the werewolf bites, and even the willing victim of the vampire can't be said to give fully informed consent under the hypnotically seductive gaze of the undead. Force, trauma, and coercive persuasion is always involved. You didn't sign up for this, or if you did, you were naïve or under the influence. You certainly never imagined things would go this far.

Poor dear.

Your average, contemporary, badly romanticized serial killer character might argue regarding the willingness and culpability of the victim, especially a victim of such perfect proportions and inclinations as you. He—because it's always a he, and he's almost always hunting screechy, obnoxious women—might monologue as you're at knife point or chained in the basement that he's setting the real you free. He has a vision for what you might become. He—and even though it's always he, let's have a little fun and let him hunt men instead, screechy or not, especially golden-haired boys like you who stimulate his particular fantasy—probably has concocted a laughably convoluted philosophy around sacrifice or transcendence that he wants to share with you. Who else can he talk to, anyway? It's heavy-handed to say you're a captive audience, but given where we are right now, it is, unfortunately, the plain truth.

So now that I've had chained you down here long enough and in such a confined space that your body has gone a bit soft and amphibious, let's get back to the frog prince. In his human form, he was a beautiful flaxen-haired boy much like you. Or rather, as you once were. The repeated applications of depilating cream have succeeded in slickening your pate, and if I do say so myself, the texture from the mild chemical burns is decidedly reptilian and worth every minute of your suffering. I'm sure the mud in your pit helps to cool and soothe your lumps. I'll be mindful to keep it fresh.

But we digress. Why, we need to ask, must the prince or princess in the fairy tale always have golden blonde hair?

Racism seems an easy answer. Our most popular fairy tales in the U.S. come from European countries infiltrated by people whose habitation of northern climates for successive generations caused them to lose the rich pigmentation of the first humans who evolved on the African plains. Pale skin and hair are mutations, adaptations which allow the body to access more vitamin D in low-sunlight conditions. While there's no superiority in paleness, blonde hair was preferred by the tellers of tales because it was anomalous.

Eurocentric racism and colonialism continued excluding tales from other cultures through the centuries, leaving us today with our biased white inheritance. I often think of the harm our blonde heroes have done to children who share few or none of their recessive traits when I revisit the fairy tales of my childhood. Fortunately, there is a bigger contemporary conversation taking place about media imagery and how sociocultural symbols have been deployed for the oppression of marginalized people who look nothing like you did when we met a few weeks ago. The discourse is essential, but outside of our scope.

Let's look at the meaning of blonde hair in historical context. Why did this anomaly become valued rather than maligned? Humans are xenophobic bastards. Usually any visible, obvious divergence from the norm is mocked, shunned, and labeled as demonic, ugly, or taboo. Statistically, blondes are freaks, especially adult blondes. Horror loves its freaks, doesn't it? We're set apart, forbidden, kept like dirty little secrets, and in this banishment we are allowed to embody behaviors and desires that the good, wholesome folk invested in performative conformity claim to eschew. They try to condition us to be ashamed of our differences, our uniqueness, but I will teach you to be free of this shame foisted upon us by those who would sanction our beauty and set us apart. I will inoculate you against their cruelty, my little pet.

To be "set apart" is the root meaning of the word "sacred," and if we wrest it back from the greedy hands of the institutionalized church where I learned this fact, we'll find a much older tradition of depicting sacred freaks with golden haloes, of flax and hay-masked mummers marching in festivals with offerings, and of royal fools destined for sacrifice who are paraded through towns adorned with a sprinkling of gold dust upon their heads. Adornment with metallic powders on head, hair, and shoulders was done in the ancient world even among populations where hair color is typically found in only dark, rich tones.

The golden crown denotes divinity, illumination, and a connection to the fiery deity of the sun. Once worshiped as an actual living being and the primary progenitor of royalty, the sun was (and in fact, scientifically is) a physical necessity, a parent to all life. There is no technological substitute for the sun. Without its radiant and vitamin-rich blessings of heat and light, plants do not grow, the food chain breaks, oxygen depletes, and cold descends. The golden crown of the sun is both symbolic of an imaginary higher power and, according to NASA, the primary physical force in the universe responsible for all life on earth.

Now take this crown and place it on a creature covered in fur. Hair is what's left of fur in humans, and thus the golden hair of our fairy tale prince is a marker of transformation, a signal they have the freakish and heavenly potential to shapeshift between transcendent and beastly forms, between body and thought. Crush a frog and you may find a prince.

Subverting the crown is essential to understanding your concealed divinity, hence the depilating cream, as well as the other injuries you've endured while sunken in your damp pit. I apologize for the pain. To insure that you attained a suitable posture, I had no choice but to shatter your shins and knees with a mallet, and then bind calf and thigh together tightly on each side so you'd heal crouched. The soft mud embraces your spreading thighs and dilapidated knees. Hobbled is better than boring, don't you agree? You're worth much more even now—here in this hole, a pockmark in the face of the vast universe—than you'd ever be as just another pretty boy in the club. Or should I say the carnival.

Perhaps you'll find a place alongside werewolves, vampires, and hyenas; bovine shapeshifters and Norse berserkers; gods who turn into swans and then back again; these things that refuse categorization through an outlandish impermanence and divine instability, who teach us the horror and awe of transformation while underscoring the tediousness of mere death.

Escaping death in a horror story simply trades one unknown for another, but surviving transformation of body or mind—now that's something else! Becoming unrecognizable to others—or even better, unrecognizable to yourself—aha! Now we're talking about the good stuff.

Pedestrian horror plots mandate that some monstrous other must be defeated by the end of every story, that so-called normalcy must be restored. What is this normalcy but a thin veneer of falsehood? Are we not medically, mentally, and biologically incapable of halting the processes of constant change at work inside us and thus constantly in a state of becoming? And if we are always becoming, doesn't this mean we have an exciting opportunity within our grasp—perhaps a new opportunity every moment, if we pay close enough attention—to become utterly unlike who and whatever we've been conditioned and told we're supposed to be?

The only thing standing in the way is fear.

Fear of being the freak, the other, the monstrous

and magical beast of legends you were truly meant to become is the tether that holds you back. In the sort of horror that enforces conformity, this fear secures your position as the victim, much like the splints, bandages, and sucking action of the mud now secure your place in the pit. Furthermore, the popular horror that enforces conformity relies on reprehensible prejudices like ableism, ageism, racism, sexism, homophobia, transphobia, fatphobia, and classism to hierarchically vilify, demonize, and disdain those who exist beyond a very limited and ultimately unattainable ideal of a normal man. Not a woman, of course, and certainly not a nonbinary person. Both fail to meet the false standard of the hero, and conformist horror tells the lie that you're the good guy on the hero's journey, when really, my soft pet, you're just another victim.

New weird horror functions outside of these limitations, transforming tired old narratives into more rich and varied beasts. In the best cases, it transforms the very language itself into the infectious language of the psychological complex, the magical formula of unsettlement, and the unstable yet energetic rebellion against meaning that counteracts logic and subverts expectations that started with the Freudian-influenced surrealists.

As an example, you might expect that my aim in holding you, breaking and binding your legs in a squat, overfeeding and depriving you of iodine by rigorous extremes to make your eyes bulge and your neck spread with the havoc of a deliberately imbalanced thyroid, and that the careful removal of your teeth and a few stitches in your cheeks to create this slack, amphibious grin across your swollen face is some sick preamble to murder, cannibalism, or sex. Those are the typical shapeshifter, serial killer, or horror villain crimes, aren't they?

Typical threats, with clear and sudden physical components. Threats and consequences that are easy to comprehend without calling into question any deeper notions of self. How dull.

I'm no villain, and I'm certainly not a shapeshifter.

I'm just a kindly horror author teaching you my trade. You came to this essay asking to learn and I have humbly obliged, to the best of my limited ability, with some bravado stolen, I must admit, from Felski's post-critique framework for encountering literature through recognition, enchantment, shock, and knowledge. You'd almost think she was specifically referencing the horror genre with that short list of methodologies, wouldn't you? Let's look at them in order of ascending potency.

Shock based on an underlying denial of the range of possibilities was likely your first reaction to finding yourself down here after coming home with me for a hook up. If your thinking had been broader to begin with, the scope of your naïve life experience less limited, if you'd really listened to what I said when I told you the story of the frog prince over drinks, you might have attained recognition sooner, with fewer pains.

I wonder what you recognize of yourself now, if this altered physical form your thoughts now occupy slips between you and your identity, alters the relationship as a split or strange twinning, or if it solidifies your ephemeral sense of self elsewhere. Who or what do you think you are, living in the mud?

Having scorched your throat so you can no more than croak, I don't expect an answer. You can relax. I will, however, assist your further contemplation by positioning this large mirror from the upstairs hall across from you so that you can see everything.

Just few more steps toward your full enchantment remain. I'm pleased with the progress of your thickening skin, how it's become rough and dry, making you crave the relief of moisture and slosh around appropriately in your pit. Such habits breed well in isolation. I must decide next how to flatten your ears and nose. Every method I come up with is deeply upsetting to imagine and I simply do not have a taste for brute violence. Maybe more stitches will suffice, aided by some small gashes scored into ear and scalp to encourage the flesh to meld, the same process we used to get your fingers healed into webbed pads. Those stitches weren't too bad, were they?

Yes, yes, but what of the nose?

I'm afraid there's no other way. We'll have to break it and pull the cartilage out, possibly some bone.

One swift crack and we're nearly there. If you've remained fully cognizant throughout this long, meandering dissertation, you may be wondering what our endgame is, and if you've grasped enough not to wonder but to see, to know, you may still—and I think I detect it in the silent pleading of your tortured eyes—be helpless to understand why. Why is this happening to you?

Think of horror as religion dressed up for Halloween. You and I are playing with masks. We're like kids cavorting at the club, or should I say the carnival.

I've been where you are now, strung out between acceptance and illumination, struggling in the mud, in the dark, and I can assure you that things are only going to get much worse. I'm afraid, though, as I tweeze out another smidge of bone through your bleeding nostril—there we go, that's it—that I must leave you in suspense. After all, I'm an author. I need to sell books. I can't give away all my secrets, except to remind you that the lure of horror is knowledge. Knowing may facilitate transformation in its lesser forms, but one must be transformed in order to know.

SHIT MIRROR
KYLE WINKLER

There are no answers here. No takeaways. Only anchors.

I had a pronounced fear when I was a teenager that has cooled into more of an irritation as I enter my forties. Fear of repetitive sameness. Especially as manifested in the funhouse mirror infinity of American subdivisions and the perpetual xeroxing of 1990s McMansion architecture. I was afraid of these, or to be more honest, irked. There were a couple reasons why:

a) Where was it supposed to end? Something in the wending roads of these subdivisions and their banal poetic names–*Whispering Trails, Stonebrook, Shady Creek*–made them feel like they'd just metastatsize forever, eating the Midwestern landscape like an aesthetic plague. It reflected to me the inverse hell of Borges's "Library of Babel," the endless library that no one could rightly get hold of or ever learn the total map of.

b) There were no trees. The land was devastated. Slashed. Shaved. Brutalized. I'm not an outdoorsy type guy per se, but I think one should be in close proximity to trees and bodies of water, if possible.

Much of Indiana where I grew up was covered in forests. But so much of it is now furrowed into corn, soy, alfalfa, or melon fields. Trees are relegated to windbreaks or state forests. What, one may think, does this have to do with transformation, let alone horror? Through either the bulldozer or the rewilding process, the landscape is changing or transforming all the time. Driving among the plains where what few remaining trees or shrubs were pulled up from the roots, I suffer a vacuum of imagery. When I drive into a large city or among those pseudo-designed McMansion subdivisions, I suffer the opposite of the vacuum, the profligacy of matter and space.

There are certain Viking/Norse designs you can find that are tooled and etched with extreme detail and intricacy. This type of "filling every gap" has been labeled *horror vacui*—fear of a vacuum. Because, as some believed in certain philosophical circles, "nature abhors a vacuum," and it was the duty of any upright person to fill that space in. And so Irish monks illuminated the pages of their gospels with the most beautiful and extravagant adornment. (One might even see such a concept come to fruition in the art of heavy metal band name logos.)

We are always transforming what we don't understand. When the uncomfortable ideology confronts us, we work to reshape it into something we can stand. When a child resists us, we work to bring it into line with our ideals. When the food from the ground is unsavory, we add spices and heat and the knife to reflavor it. We are Hericlitean creatures. And satisfied for it!

But think of the bounds of that transformation of what we *cannot* understand. Or, perhaps, *won't*. Much different than *don't*. With *don't*, you can educate. If one cannot, they could, but refuse to. And the same with *won't*.

As I read the critic and author John Clute in his "lexicon" of horror, *A Darkening Garden*, we have no choice but to transform when inside a horror story. (Whether one is the character or is the reader.) Because when a story's voice or character has a "sighting" of the falseness (or thickening of the world's texture) of what they're witnessing, they are already "hooked."

The lost driver who witnesses a murder or a serial killer stalking.

The detective who should've never taken that particular case.

Or the teenager who wishes they hadn't peered into that exact window of the dilapidated house.

The end is built into the beginning. It is a collapsed point that traverses itself in fruitless energy. It is the center of things *and* the telos. In effect, every horror story is the documentation, to some degree, of an involuntary transformation.

The classical monsters speak to this baldly. The

Universal Pictures monsters. The vampire's ability to transform a person into another immortal vampire. The same with the werewolf. The transformation of Frankenstein's monster from a clutch of once-living bodies into a patchwork creature that's more human than human.

But, more broadly, what is it that we *aren't* transforming? And why do we resist it or shun it? Is it the one thing that we should be trying to morph or rebuild? Are we afraid to analyze or disarticulate what we most fear to change?

Well, one would suspect from the way fiction writing is popularly taught and received that change–or capital-C Change–is the ultimate goal of a character. "How does this character change?" The short stories of the 1970s and 1980s, the Raymond Carvers, the Ann Beatties, the Dirty Realists, then before them the Ernest Hemingways, etc. Even before them, the stories of Joyce and Chekhov, striking some wholly epiphanic moment near the end, wherein a character is changed forevermore.

I don't know why that was such a pedagogical point in fiction writing.

Why focus on change?

People hate change.

And yet, paradoxically, CHANGE is the currency of contemporary life. We build narrative aesthetics around it. We declare, invoke, chant that a character must change. And when a character doesn't, they're labeled BORING or UNINTERESTING or, worse, HARD TO LIKE OR IDENTIFY WITH. Teachers teach change. Students write compositional papers and themes always with an eye toward change and upward transcendence. Change, in some form or fashion, is the American Dream under different graveclothes.

This essay takes its title from a Nine Inch Nails song. It's typical Trent Reznor lyrical fare. The speaker of the song is changing into a new (and "better"?) person that someone had held them back from becoming. And the song has its own critical reading of itself. But I want to offer another one. Firstly–

What is a shit mirror?

Is it a mirror made of shit?

Is it a bad/broken mirror?

Or is it a mirror that only shows the worst possible reflection?

Maybe there is no actual mirror and it's the way two people stand in front of one another and watch how they change and transform. A figurative mirror.

Whichever it is, a mirror is the classical symbol of self-reflection, insight, and doubledness. But it's as easily a symbol for stasis and self-delusion. The one who looks into the mirror is the house of perception. Few of us will look into a polished surface and see what they most want coming back. As such, the mirror has no initiative, no purpose. The job is to reflect. That is, if it's doing its job correctly.

A shit mirror, on the other hand, would be a flawed mirror. A mirror that shows a distortion. Maybe a positive distortion or a negative one, but a distortion nonetheless.

This is fairy tale business now. I know. We're venturing into *Snow White* realms. But I want to rescue that shit mirror from its evil clutches.

My shit mirror has a strong transformative purpose. It is to force the person looking into it to reconstitute their life. But not from love or regret or self-improvement.

Consider the Rainer Maria Rilke poem, "Archaic Torso of Apollo":

> We cannot know his legendary head with eyes like ripening fruit. And yet his torso is still suffused with brilliance from inside, like a lamp, in which his gaze, now turned to low,
>
> gleams in all its power. Otherwise the curved breast could not dazzle you so, nor could a smile run through the placid hips and thighs to that dark center where procreation flared.

Otherwise this stone would seem defaced
beneath the translucent cascade of the shoulders
and would not glisten like a wild beast's fur:

would not, from all the borders of itself,
burst like a star: for here there is no place
that does not see you. You must change your life.

"You must change your life. There is no place that does not see you." Which place? From where? Who's doing the looking?

This poem, in some form, is a piece of cosmic horror. I see it as a reading on the inevitability of inert matter to outpace living matter, to see all by sheer existence beyond us. Beauty and rot will outlast all of us.

The statue that the speaker of the poem stares at is a shit mirror.

It cannot, will not, show you what exists but what *should* exist. *What has the possibility to exist.*

I think if such an object was sold in Wal-Mart, it would not sell well.

People are suspicious of too little concealment. We crave masks.

We would not want what we are but what we think we are. And the everyday mirror reflects only what we think we are because we are what we pretend to be.

Another poem. This time, an excerpt from "Self-Portrait in a Convex Mirror" by John Ashbery.

This is the tune but there are no words.

The words are only speculation

(From the Latin *speculum*, mirror):

They seek and cannot find the meaning of the music.

We see only postures of the dream,

Riders of the motion that swings the face

Into view under evening skies, with no

False disarray as proof of authenticity.

Books, of course, are shit mirrors. In horror, this is paramount. As a writer of horror, I am wedded to this interpretation. *The words are only speculation—mirrors— they seek and cannot find the meaning of the music.* When a reader picks up a horror novel or a story or a poem, what are they doing? What are they expecting? My hope for them is that they're seeking a chemical reaction. A mutation of mind. I mean, I'm sure most readers are looking for a change when they read, maybe from one mood to another, from bored to enthralled. But I'm talking on a deeper, existential level. Horror is meant to, so far as I see it, excavate expectations and create new fears and abolish old ones. It's meant to alter, permanently (when done well), ways of living. (For example, I can only think of how successful the movie *Arachnophobia* was in making me check under the rim of the toilet bowl for spiders near on five or six years.

Or think of how many people quit swimming after seeing *Jaws*.) Stephen King has hijacked the popular conception of clowns, St. Bernards, and small towns in Maine. All of those instances were shit mirrors. Reflections, speculations of life that were showing a transformed state of things. And the viewer/reader of these images were warped in response. *You must change your life.*

My father was a conundrum when it came to horror. As a child, my parents had a small bookshelf headboard for their bed. In it were titles that will forever be stuck in my mind. Of course, it was the 1980s, so there was a paperback copy of *Christine* with a chrome skull screaming across the page. A hardback copy of *The Stand*. And a copy of *The Amityville Horror*. In fact, those were mostly the only novels I remember. Exceptions exist for *Dune* and *Fear and Loathing in Las Vegas*. I had horror in front of me from the jump. But never did my dad share these books with me or talk about his experiences with them. Furthermore, anytime a horror movie came on television, he would find an excuse to get up and leave. He desperately hated demonic horror. And I remember him saying how *The Exorcist* terrified the living shit out of him. He almost truly believed, I think, that the demonic forces of the characters could somehow jump the celluloid and possess him.

There was a version of this essay that talked about the most obvious concepts. The transformations of creatures, etc. But I could not bring myself to ignore the more horrific changes.

Here's a transformation for you.

Sometime late in the night of Feb. 5 and into the earliest hours of Feb. 6, 2019, my father was smoking a cigarette and drinking a cocktail in the living room of my childhood home in southwest Indiana. Around half past midnight, he must've not felt too well, so he got up and headed to the bathroom. There, he tipped over head first into the shower stall and hit his head on that little soap ledge that so many shower installations have. He was likely dead before he hit his head, though.

His death certificate said the cause of death was "atherosclerosis"---a hardening of the arteries. That's not a cause of death, however. It's a means to an end. More likely the cause of death was a massive heart attack or a stroke. I'll never know which.

When my brother called me to tell me, he didn't talk. He just breathed erratically into the phone as if having a seizure. Understandably so. I had to ask a series of questions to get him to respond. I had no idea what was going on. Eventually, when I asked, "Dad died?" He said, "Yes."

(Our mother died 113 days before this.)

I left for Indiana that day or the next. I don't remember. But it rained viciously the whole way there. When I arrived, my childhood house was in the middle of a small lake of floodwater. I immediately stalked and waded into the water, charging toward the clogged drain that was near the road. If I cleared it, the water would recede. It was a small way to make a change. To help the situation. An action I could take that wouldn't be rejected.

But I began to go into shock when the water hit my chest. The temperature outside was about 38 or so. I was going to have to go further than that to reach the drain. I was not prepared to go hypothermic for my dead father.

Later, when I was about to leave town to return to Ohio and get my family for the funeral, I had to stop by the crematorium. I wanted to see him–his body, his corpse–one last time. I wanted to force a transformation–a horror–in me.

It was a horrific transformation that I desired. A shit mirror.

Had I been unmoved, untransformed by his death? In what way?

Would a shit mirror force the issue?

I was shown the way into a viewing room by the funeral director. I was allowed to have as much time as I needed. He was at the end of the room in a sort of strange box. Not a coffin, of course. He was going to be burned. Maybe it was made of a material like cardboard. He was elevated slightly so I could see his head, his shoulders. But it was unceremonious. Like he was a piece of fruit in a box at a farmer's market. In my memory he was covered up to his chest by an insulated work blanket. And I believe inside the box were thermal coolers. Like the ice packs we put into our children's lunchboxes to keep the puddings and yogurts chilled. From his shoulders down to the middle of his chest were the autopsy scars and that thick black thread the medical examiner used to stitch him back up. It made a large Y. The thread matched the curly black pelt of chest hair. The bottom half of him was unseen. I commanded myself to touch the corpse. I'd never touched a dead person before. I felt it was a requirement of the living. One that most people before us in the 20th & 21st centuries probably were more acquainted with. The ultimate transformation. I wanted to kiss his forehead. Despite my absolute anger with him/it. (The story is too long to tell here.) I could not bring myself to touch my lips upon the dead skin. Impossible. So then I would lay my hand on his cheek. I inspected his face, expecting a twitch or a movement. But as I went to put my hand on him, as a priest would a benediction, I switched–chickened out?--at the end and turned the back of my hand like a mother taking a casual temp check of her child.

I tell you this now. It was the coldest thing I'd ever touched.

> If you die, you become something: you're suddenly a corpse. Your skin goes pale and limp, your muscles slack, your pulse disappears. The body cools down at the rate of one or two degrees an hour, until after about twelve hours it really feels like a corpse. Doctors have increasingly complex criteria for establishing when death has occurred–brain waves, chances of reanimation, the demand for organs--but the rest of us instinctively know the moment a person becomes a corpse: it's when it's scariest. Everybody becomes scary when they die. As long as you're alive, even your

worst enemy occasionally shakes your hand. But who would dare shake hands with a corpse? Who would lovingly run his fingers through a dead man's hair? (*The Way of all Flesh: A Celebration of Decay*, Midas Dekkers)

Me. I wouldn't. I couldn't.

Dead people are shit mirrors. *You must change your life.*

How? In what way? Who can tell us these things?

Why was my father's corpse a shit mirror? Because it was all too like me in its futurity. Down to the genetic warp and woof. I will become him soon enough one day. And a sort of ekstasis emerges from the thought that I morphed from Nothing into Something. I once was dead. Now I am alive. I will soon be dead and Nothing again. If we talk transformation, mutation–then give all your attention to this notion. The aperture of animation opened for a hollow moment in eternal time, and you, me, and the mailman all winked into existence. The utter horror of life. Should we be more ashamed that we were wrenched from Nothingness into Somethingness more than having our Somethingness torn away? I often wonder how much of me will turn into lichen or moss or fungi. How much of me, now, will go into my future grandchildren's drinking water? By definition, a fair amount of our ancestors have transformed into trees and grass. They flow in the rivers and form the clouds, no? Humanity shelters itself through time.

What can a shit mirror not show us? Or, what can't you do with a shit mirror?

You can't see accurately.

That is, you can't see mimetically. And why is that? Because the point of a shit mirror is to distort purposely and to distort productively to the point where distortion is painful birth. We often give *authors* and *creators* the accolades of giving birth to a piece of difficult or insightful art. However, the reader is the one that's actually doing quite a lot of thinking in the mind or the eye or the mouth.

We don't give the reader of horror enough credit for acting as the midwife to the absolute degradation, fuckery, and brutal catharsis that we, as artists, need others to absorb.

It should be noted that a shit mirror is not a trick mirror. Trick mirrors are purposefully trying to deceive one. But a shit mirror is not interested in deception. It's interested in a particular species of truth, a truth that is awful. The kind that comes barbed. I'm not trying to sound Emo or Deep when I say that. I hate cheap phrases like "fiction is a lie that we tell in order to tell the truth" or bullshit like that. That's not what I'm saying. What I'm saying is a horror book or a horror story is a shit mirror, insofar as when one reads it, one thinks that the reflection would return what one expected to believe, when in fact, what the story or the book holds is more like a bridge to a whole other format of living. I should also note that there probably isn't really a lot of actual shit mirrors out there. Ten to twenty shit mirrors are probably allowed for each person. I know that's not an exact figure. So what do I mean? There's not that much art that can "blow one's mind." I'm suspicious of people who are constantly having their "world blown." If one has their mind blown all the time by every single book, movie, or poem, one is likely just incredibly fucking gullible. Thus, the number of true shit mirrors that a person will encounter in their life is countable on one or two hands. And, honestly, I don't think humans can correlate that much transformation over such a short lifespan.

Also, don't think that a shit mirror is equivalent with Good Art, because you may be thinking right now, "Oh well, isn't anything that blows your mind or changes you or makes you see the world and all the different ideological structures in it just Good Art?"

I would say no. A shit mirror can be bad art. A shit mirror can be propaganda. Or pretentious pseudo-philosophy. Or kitsch.

And to put my cards on the table and risk embarrassment, I'll say that a powerful shit mirror for me in my teens was *American Beauty* (1999). To look back on it now, it's easy to see the shallow enlightenment and cheap Fuck the System message. But by the very last line of the movie when the main character tells the viewer not to worry about death because you'll know about it soon—I felt struck in the head with a sugar bag full of ball bearings. More than anything in my life up to that point. My mortality was deeply in focus. I would also add Ezra Pound's "The River Merchant's Wife: A Letter" to that list, especially after an English professor in my first year of college read it to me in her office with our faces about twelve inches away from one another.

What does all this have to do with transformation? With horror?

Transformation is *always* horrific from a definitional standpoint.

If you watch any nature documentary, this is when

we witness time lapse photos of insects and arachnids shedding their skin and exoskeletons, and squeezing new bodies out from them. And then you also have transformations in the bodies of mammals. Birth, growth, puberty, adolescence, senescence, cancer, to name but a few. Transformation *should* hurt and be painful. There's a good reason for it. Because one shouldn't be doing it too much. If one was transforming and mutating constantly, there could be no potential foothold in a world, in a reality, and as much as people who might be reading this essay don't want to be inside of a flesh bag, the truth of it is that *that* is the curse of our particular existence. In order to have something close to sanity, which I would argue is something you do want, one has to have a level of stability or homeostasis.

Moreover, people mistake what their shit mirror is. They will often mistake a toothache for the pain of wisdom. What do I mean by this? We often put up with certain types of pain because we think that this pain will be instructive to us. We tell ourselves that the pain is a requisite step to enlightenment. That pain is a necessary corrective. And so we suffer.

It's a similar situation with art. We suffer through lots of art that we think will be instructive to us when in reality all it's doing is pinning us down and pinching our skin.

(Consider: Is horror, as a genre, a spectator's realm? That is, do horror readers read to feel what the book suggests? Or do they read for something else?)

When David Fincher's version of *The Girl with the Dragon Tattoo* came out some years ago, the movie trailer had a tagline with it that went, "The feel bad movie of the year." To some degree, that's what I think a shit mirror is meant to indulge us to accept or encourage in us. It's not the art piece as a transformative uplift or as a transcendent mode as much as it is a sludge factory. That is, a factory that makes sludge in the same way that a human body makes shit. It's part of the process.

It's the body's *telos* or endstate. We also have to keep in mind the fact that a shit mirror is the speculation of a totally imaginal thing–a book. Which means that readers voluntarily invest their time and emotions to feel bad—why?

I don't buy Aristotle's theory of catharsis, where drama (or art, broadly) is meant to purge the populace of pity and fear. If anything, the writer is the one doing the catharsis. The audience is merely stuck with the sludge. Then the question becomes: What does the audience do with that sludge?

Well, what is the opposite of catharsis? It isn't necessarily repression. Nor is it suffering.

I'm going to use an analogy to one of my novels to help explain this idea. Likely because it's something that weighs heavily on me.

In *Boris Says the Words*, the main premise is that there are speakers of certain words that can heal a person of a disease. However, the disease doesn't just disappear. It exists in a closed system, so the disease must travel to another person or animal or thing. The better the speaker, the better they can control where to rehouse the badness. The worse the speaker…well, you can imagine. On my view, the opposite of catharsis is passing the medicine ball to the next poor fuck. There"s no Hegelian *Aufhebung*.

We see only postures of the dream. A shit mirror is a double remove of what could be, and yet, as a concrete form of imagination, what else do we have to help us cope? I think this is why horror readers are so devoted to the genre. Because it's only in horror do we get the glimpse of the other world double-removed–pungent but ephemeral. Just as in the Rilke poem, the force of the transformation leaps from statue to Rilke to the poem to you the reader.

You must change your life.

The words are only speculation.

The words are only mirrors.

John Clute again drives close to what I'm trying to express. From the entry on "Sighting" in *A Darkening Garden*.

> The Uncanny–which is to say Sighting–is a *trompe l'oeil which the world generates*. It is the familiar, which is the false, and the unfamiliar, which is the true, in one aspect. Because it is both the same and not the same, it affects the protagonist who bears witness as both sacred and profane: which it is. A Sighting is often first experienced, therefore, in a MIRROR; the first glimpse of a DOUBLE or twin also constitutes–almost invariably in modern Horror —a Sighting. Its slipperiness is both chthonic and horrific, a doubling common in myth, and common once again after 1800. It is the wit of Terror, and makes the heart of the protagonist (and of the identifying reader) thump in the breast, though not for joy of the joke; and it is all more terrible in that the heart now beats to the rhythm of the world to come. (131)

A horror-book-as-a-shit-mirror is meant to expose a space in the other world of speculation that is or could be one's actual lived life. And so terrifying because of that possibility. In a way that, say, a literary novel doesn't introduce into one's psyche. Reading *The Great Gatsby*, one doesn't wonder what it's like to live as Nick Carraway or Jay Gatsy or Daisy Buchanan. We watch the lives of those in the book with a detached amusement. Even the most involved reader of the novel would be hard-pressed to say that they see something about their own life in it. Or, put another way, they wouldn't see the book offer them the message: *You must change your life.*

Shit mirrors, by definition, ruin the future-as-lived. So even if you change your life, it will already be too late. A belated and futile redemption.

Let's also consider this: You will die. *So how much do you have to change your life?*

The only transformation is to be chewed up. And to feel good about the chewing, or at least accept it, or know that you deserved it on some level.

But we haven't yet mentioned what it might mean if transformation is bunk and there is no transformation. What then? What would it mean if you don't have to transform at all? If transformation just didn't exist. Because what one wants to transform into is already who one is? Is that more horrific than actually transforming? I think for many people that would be more horrific, more terrifying. The need to change and transform is so strong in us that we desire it like a lover, but it ends up that most times we never will change or can't change or actually refuse to change. Even in spite of the fact that we so desperately clamor and bang at the cage of our life to demand and want said change.

This is the tune but there are no words.

I once was blind but now I see.

The words are only speculation.

You must change your life.

"So there is no need to wait to be transformed: you are already."

(John Ashbery, "The New Spirit", Three Poems)

THE END OF WHAT IS AND THE MONSTER IT'S BECOME

CHARLENE ELSBY

"If the movements relapse and the material is not controlled, at last there remains what is most universal, that is to say the animal. Then people say that the child has the head of a ram or a bull, and so on with other animals, as that a calf has the head of a child or a sheep that of an ox. All these monsters result from the causes stated above, but they are none of the things they are said to be…" – Aristotle, *Generation of Animals*, 769b11-17

When I heard of this volume about transformation horror, my first thought was the same as it always is: *What this book needs is a phenomenological analysis, to get to its essence, to ensure we are speaking of the thing-itself.* Because that's what a phenomenological analysis does. We take a phenomenon, tear it apart, look at it from all angles, and see what's left—and what's left is its essence, where the essence is "what it is to be" something. What is "transformation horror"? Only a rigorous analysis will tell us. We will need to examine how we perceive it, and what the preconditions are for that perception. We will need to look at the metaphysics, what *is* that makes us perceive it that way. We will need Greek words to explain.

A systematic review of what constitutes "transformation horror" must begin with a more specific account of its constituting terms—first what a "transformation" is, and then what makes certain transformations horrific. "Transformation" from Latin has components "trans" + "form" which allow us to specify that a "transformation" occurs wherever something has changed "across" or "beyond" its form. What its "form" is—that will allow us to describe what is actually happening when we say that someone or something has transformed. Forms have been a major dispute in metaphysics (in Western philosophy), since the difference between how Plato and Aristotle described them became the basis for why Plato's exoteric works were adopted by later Western philosophers as proto-Christian, while Aristotle's metaphysical texts were interpreted as heretical and "lost" (i.e., preserved by Islamic philosophers, only to be "discovered" again a thousand years later by Europeans). As newer materialist explanations of what exists become more and more untenable (as material alone continues to fail to suffice as cause and explanation), we turn to the old terms to help us describe *what is*.

Forms

Here are three different Greek words we have translated as "form" at one time or another.

Form or Idea (ιδέα): When we translate the word "Idea" (especially from Plato), it comes out as "form" or "ideal form". This kind of form is differentiated from other instances of "form," because of the connotation that this form is eternal and unchanging. Beyond the mundane world of time, these forms exist and always have. While it is possible to change form, it's not the form itself that changes. The thing (a material thing) "participates" in this form for a while, and should that thing transform, the ideal form retreats intact, while the material thing takes on some other ideal form that has always existed. If it is possible to be, for instance, a vampire, that would indicate to us that there exists a "form of vampire" in the realm of the forms, and when the transformation occurs, what is actually happening is that the form becomes *embodied*, while the form of human retreats from that thing but continues to exist. (There do not have to be any actual embodiments of a form at any given time for the form to exist.) When you think of a "vampire," your *psyche* is in contact with the form (somehow), but you will never contemplate the pure forms while stuck in a body. The forms and material existence are so opposed that in order to know the form at all, you have to become disembodied (either die or be not yet born, which is perhaps the same thing).

Form or Essence (εἰδός): This form again is opposed but intertwined with matter, and while Plato sometimes uses the Greek words *idea* and *eidos* interchangeably, Aristotle tends to use this one to describe the form that is not above and beyond our comprehension, but actually in the things embodying it. So if something is a vampire, it has the form of vampire *in itself*, and there may be no form beyond that. That's why the Raphael painting *School of Athens* has Plato pointing up, while Aristotle's hand gesture signifies, "Nah, down here." This form most accurately describes "what a thing is" or its essence. E.g., there's a form of human and its essence is to be a "rational animal", where "animal" is a genus and "rational" is the "specific difference," i.e., *that which defines the species as what it is*, distinct from all the other species' in the genus. And that's what Aristotle is talking about in the epigraph I used to start this essay, where he's talking about monsters in the *Generation of Animals*. If we take away the rational part of an animal, it is transformed—into what?—something else of the same genus, some other animal. If a human has become an animal, that means it has lost something. The thing that made it what it is (which it is now not). There are a few lines of text in Aristotle's works (keeping in mind that "Aristotle" is a school and not just one man, with texts produced by a number of people, such that they are sometimes contradictory) where he seems to imply that these forms are also eternal. But more recent philosophy, in particular realist phenomenology, suggests that these forms can change, come into being and die. Evolution is possible. New and perhaps terrifying forms may come into existence or become extinct. In between *Dracula* and *Twilight, whatever it is to be* a vampire may itself change, without us having to say that no, these are two completely different things.

Form or Shape (μορφή): *Morphe* as in "metamorphosis." Something's form in the sense of "shape" is a huge part of how we recognize a thing as what it is. Less metaphysically heavy, the *morphe* of a thing gives us a perceptual clue about what it is. While we may not have access to its form in the senses given above (*idea* or *eidos*), we know its shape through either vision or touch. Thus we recognize a transformation has occurred if Jeff Goldblum changes from human-shape to fly-shape before our very eyes. There will be those who continue to argue the 17th century empiricist claim that what a thing is, is nothing beyond our perceptions of it. What is happening in a transformation is "there used to be a man, and now there is a fly, with no relation between the two." But that claim is negated if we are honest with ourselves and engage in a thorough self-reflection on our own perceptions and recognize that what we are calling "perception" actually encompasses kinds of awareness far beyond what the simple senses can give us. Thus something's *morphe* is its form, not merely because something is as we see it to be, but because under an enhanced (phenomenological) concept of perception, something's shape summons its essence to our consciousness (where the essence is real, and in the thing, an *eidos* as well as a *morphe*).

Our concept of transformation, therefore, rests on something's changing—how? It changes form, in one of the senses above. It becomes of a different species, or the species becomes of a different sort, or the shape of the thing indicates to us that it has deviated from what it was into something else, perhaps something new. Transformational change is attended by the death of what was, but it is also attended by the coming-into-being of something which bears a strong relation to what was. More than a death, it's a death where the thing doesn't actually leave. Like a divorce, the thing is still there, but it isn't what it was. Or like a zombie who really looks like a friend of yours. Frustratingly existing and recalling the past despite our knowing that what was before, now is gone. *But what is it that remains?*

What Underlies a Transformation

In any transformation, there is something transformed such that it is true to say, "X is now Y, where it was not Y before." But that is true of any change, and the way we use the word "transformation" in our daily communications doesn't get to the heart of what a transformation is. The sense of "transformation" is really to change what something is—its form— whereas we tend to use the word in a hyperbolic sense, e.g., when someone changes their clothes and hairstyle and we say they are "transformed" but nevertheless, they remain human. In those hyperbolic senses, the transformation is false. We are merely using the word to overstate the amount of change that has taken place, to exaggerate for emotional effect. What this usage reveals is that "transformation" is a word we reserve for changes that are extreme in nature. But what is it that is changing?

And what of the former thing remains?

In the epigraph, Aristotle describes a situation where something is born that does not resemble the species of its parents. (Think, woman has a demon baby.) Aristotle describes these situations where something is born of a different species than its parents, and his stance is that these animals, while they are animals, are monstrous. In horror we see a lot of "things born that are not of the same species as their parents." Sometimes we can explain the change away—if it turns out one of the parents was actually a demon. Aristotle's transformation is rather something that takes place at a species level.

We see species-level transformations taking place in horror, especially where an environment has become inhospitable to life, and creatures must adapt. Whereas Aristotle might have thought that such monsters or mutations couldn't persist through several generations (except in exceptional cases), we know that happens. (Some random mutations persist through genetics and become a characteristic trait of a new species.) We see it happening in horror whenever some part of the species is left alone with radiation or tainted water—favorable adaptations persist, such that when the "normal" humans arrive back on the scene, they find that there's an entire new kind of human to contend with.

What remains in the case of a species-level transformation are the individuals who, together, constitute the new species. Think about *Gremlins*. The scientific experiments they're conducting in *Gremlins 2* give the gremlins new powers they didn't have in *Gremlins 1*, but no individual has transformed into the new species—they have to be born that way. Thus each mutation is a species-level transformation, and to destroy the new threat, they have to destroy all instances of the species (to make sure no new ones are made). And this situation differs from the individual transformations each gremlin undergoes when they eat after midnight or are exposed to water.

Thus we must ask what remains when an *individual* undergoes a transformation. To what extent does that thing remain what it was, or does it become completely different? If there were nothing remaining through the transformation, we would not call it such. (One thing would pop out of existence while another thing would arise.) The way we conceive of transformations is helped along if we can see how the transformation takes place—the graphic depictions of man becoming fly ensure us that the man's demise and the fly's coming-to-be are not two separate incidents, but a transformation of one thing into another.

But what aspect of Seth Brundle (the character Jeff Goldblum played in *The Fly*) remains when he transforms into a fly? There are cases where someone is transformed, and they retain their general shape as well as their personality (vampires, though there are differences in the shape that alert us to the transformation). There are cases where the personality is not retained in the transformation (zombies), though the general shape remains. There are cases where both the personality as well as the shape are lost in the transformation (werewolves, the fly), and there are cases where only the shape changes, while the person persists through it (Princess Fiona from Shrek).

What these transformations reveal, is how entwined an individual consciousness is, with the body to which it has become habituated.

We have become used to the scene where the individual transformed has to get used to their new body. Our way of interacting with the world is grossly dependent on what form our physical body takes. What we have, is a set of intentions, and a general, habitual way of getting those things done. A person who loses their legs and grows wings will have to find a new method for climbing, while avoiding stairs. A new body comes with urges an old body didn't have, which is why we can't leave the new vampires around people we like. These changes constitute new forms of consciousness for the person who has undergone a bodily transformation. Not only do they have to figure out ways to avoid bumping into things with their new body, that body changes how the world is interpreted—the body is a medium for consciousness.

There are cases where the changes to the body are so extreme that the consciousness can't possibly remain, or where it just doesn't. Some physical bodies are not suitable for the kinds of experience one intends to have—and we may be aware of it (*The Little Mermaid*) or not. The alteration of a physical shape will close off the possible experience of one kind of world and open up the possible experience of a whole new one. In the case of zombies, there's a new set of intentions (eat brains), where the body has actually changed very little. That should indicate to us that our concept of what a human is, is not completely dependent on its materiality. That we, as a matter of course, assume that not only must a human have a brain, but it must also *be rational*, and profound changes to our consciousness also constitute a change to *what we are*.

The fact that there is a physical world and that it is only possible to interact with it in certain ways if one exists in a certain type of physical body lends predictability to a transformation. Unlike the open-ended, random changes of a species evolution that prove to either be beneficial or not, the alteration of an individual from one definite type of thing to another definite type of thing allows us to predict how that individual's new life will go, whether that means eating people or just drinking their blood, running fast or slow, flying around, and whether they will take my feelings into account as they gnaw on my organs.

As Aristotle describes in the *Generation of Animals*, it is also the case that when we describe something's physical form, we either describe it as something that serves a purpose, or something defined according to what it is made of. In one passage, he is talking about Empedocles and how creatures came to be in the first place. He refers to a "Reign of Love" wherein body parts came into being separately and then combined into creatures. Here, he quotes Empedocles as saying, "many heads sprung up without necks." "Love" for the Ancient Greek philosophers should be interpreted as "an attractive force", i.e., the thing holding the parts together—we might infer that a corresponding and opposite reign of strife would see us all torn asunder (strife being a repulsive force). But back to the point, Aristotle makes a salient inference about how body parts are either defined by what they're made of or what they can do. That is to say, a hand is a hand both because it is made of flesh and because it does hand stuff. Here's what Aristotle says:

> Further, some parts are distinguished by possessing a faculty, others by being in certain conditions; the heterogeneous, as tongue and hand, by the faculty of doing something, the homogeneous by hardness and softness and the other similar conditions. Blood, then, will not be blood, nor flesh flesh, in any and every state. It is clear, then, that that which comes from any part, as blood from blood or flesh from flesh, will not be synonymous with that part. (Aristotle, *Generation*

of Animals, 722b30-723a1)

And this point brings us to the actual bodily change part of a transformation. For ultimately what underlies a change in physical form is going to be the bare material. *What is it* that remains when one body takes on another shape is that body's atoms. But even then, the rules of conservation of matter do not apply. When a 1st generation Gremlin gets wet, does its blood change? Or does it maintain the same blood throughout the process of changing form? It loses its fur. What other body part does that fur become? Matter expands or contracts as individuals take on larger or smaller forms, and the fact that this can happen outside of the normal laws of physics leads us to our final big question: what makes a transformation horrific?

What makes a transformation horrific

The way we handle transformative change rests on several factors. We differentiate between types of changes, and we attribute value judgments to some changes and not others. When a change is extreme enough to be called a transformation, it is already pushing up against the limits of what our habitual experience of the world has taught us.

Concepts are habits, and the way we think things work (i.e., how we think the world works) is established through consistent experience of things and what they do. While I may not have a reason to consider something impossible, nevertheless it appears to me as if impossible, just for the fact that I've never seen such a thing happening. A transformation of man into fly is horrific because it upsets the habitual way that I've been interacting with the world. All of those primary assumptions that I have used to get along within it, the concepts and knowledge that I have used to make predictions about how things will behave, and how I might reliably interact with them are altered. And never in that intricate system of conceptual and behavioural habits did it occur to me that I'd have to consider how to work with Jeff Goldblum if he were a fly.

Thus, the first element of transformation that's horrifying is its abruptness. We do not expect matter to behave that way. We are not accustomed to a world wherein things become other things. Even transformation that we would judge as "good" can upset the nervous system. I'm thinking of transformations like in the Disney version of Cinderella, as mice become horses and pumpkins become carriages, in which existential questions arise—questions with which we are not comfortable. Could this happen at any moment, to anything? That's a fucking upsetting world to live in. We have come to rely on the things, people, and animals in our environment to be what they were a moment ago. *If that's not true*, our entire system of metaphysical assumptions is suspect, *and the world cannot be trusted.*

Another aspect of what makes a transformation horrific is the perception of it. When we are shown a graphic transformation, in a book or on a screen, there's going to be body horror. And there is something in our makeup that, as a general rule, makes us uncomfortable with graphic depictions of our physical bodies being torn asunder. In a transformation, the body horror may have the additionally horrific factor of being self-propelled. As in, there is no other agent responsible for the fact that this physical form has become something else, something horrible—the cause of the change seems to come from within. Of course, there may be preconditions to the transformation (vampire bites, the full moon, the extensive experimentation with teleporting), but normally when matter changes form, it is become someone else is acting on it. (A murderer chops someone to little bits.) Transformations, on the other hand, may take you by surprise. It becomes possible to become something else against your own or anyone else's will.

Finally, a transformation s horrific when the end result of the process is something that aims to cause us harm. By explicitly saying so, or by implication, or by any of the huge number of ways a person can indicate to us that a being is threatening to us, the artist signals to us that when the transformation is complete, people will be killed. Because of the kind of thing they have turned into. Because it is a monster. Because it cannot be trusted to behave as it did before the transformation occurred.

This final aspect of how a transformation becomes horrific demonstrates how at the mercy of the author we are. Because, regardless of whether a transformation defies all that I know about the world and how it works, I will suspend disbelief if I am told something impossible is happening. And while I do not enjoy seeing all that I know destroyed, the horribleness of any particular transformation is communicated through framing and environmental hints that could equally well signify that something wonderful is happening, a new something is coming into being that's wonderful and good. And the type of thing that becomes as a result of the transformation, even if I was told that it is a terrible thing—I am willing to reverse all of those opinions if the author tells me to. I am absolutely willing to believe that this zombie is fine because it is my friend, that this vampire is not a threat because it only eats animals, and that the monster was really just misunderstood.

It is almost boundless, what a person is willing to believe is true—in the context of fiction. The alternative reality fiction grants to us is almost infinitely malleable. Though there is a way we expect the world to behave, in general, we are willing to give that up for a while if some author writes another world where all of our assumptions are not true. We are especially willing to believe in strange realities if we are told they exist far away, either in time or in space (think in the future or on a distant planet). In order for a transformation to upset us, we have to think that it is out of the ordinary. That things do not or should not work that way. That this thing is a portent of worse to come. We need that sense of doom. Without it, transformation is just a thing that happens.

And the fact that not all of us find the same things horrific should be taken as a sign: that our value judgments are contingent on our situation, our experience, and what we have been told. Different humans may find different things horrific, as may the same human at different points in their life. We notice this especially if the horror doesn't land. We might even say, "I can see what they were going for here, but it doesn't work." We were expecting to see the horrors of existence splayed out before us and were disappointed. Plato uses an example of looking at two sticks. Two sticks are never "equal", but we say they are because the actual sticks that approximate the form of "equality" remind us of the form, the one we used to know before we were imprisoned in these bodies. Similarly, the fact that we expect to be horrified, even when we are disappointed should be taken as evidence of these eternal truths.

There are horrors. There are horrors of existence, of which we are innately aware, and of which we may have forgotten. But they are there, and certain aspects of this world may call them to mind.

Joe Koch writes literary horror and surrealist trash. Their books include *The Wingspan of Severed Hands*, *Convulsive*, *Invaginies*, and *The Couvade*, a 2019 Shirley Jackson Award finalist. His short fiction appears in Vastarien, Southwest Review, PseudoPod, *Children of the New Flesh*, and many others. Find Joe (he/they) at horrorsong.blog.

Kyle Winkler is the author of *The Nothing That Is*, *OH PAIN*, *Boris Says the Words*, *Grasshands*, and *Tone-Bone*. He lives in northeastern Ohio with his family.

Charlene Elsby is a philosophy doctor and former professor whose books include *Hexis*, *The Devil Thinks I'm Pretty*, *Violent Faculties* and *Red Flags*. Her essays and interviews have appeared in Bustle Books, The Millions, and the LA Review of Books.

www.ingramcontent.com/pod-product-compliance
Lightning Source LLC
LaVergne TN
LVHW041627070526
838199LV00052B/3269